Free My Mind

An Anthology of Black and Asian Poetry

Selected by Judith Elkin and Carlton Duncan

PUFFIN BOOKS

PUFFIN BOOKS

Published by the Penguin Group
Penguin Books Ltd, 27 Wrights Lane, London W8 5TZ, England
Penguin Books USA Inc., 375 Hudson Street, New York, New York 10014, USA
Penguin Books Australia Ltd, Ringwood, Victoria, Australia
Penguin Books Canada Ltd, 10 Alcorn Avenue, Toronto, Ontario, Canada M4V 3B2
Penguin Books (NZ) Ltd, 182–190 Wairau Road, Auckland 10, New Zealand

Penguin Books Ltd, Registered Offices: Harmondsworth, Middlesex, England

First published by Hamish Hamilton Ltd 1992
Published in Puffin Books 1995
1 3 5 7 9 10 8 6 4 2

Filmset in Monophoto Bembo

Printed in England by Clays Ltd, St Ives plc

CONTENTS

BLACK FEMALE WARRIOR

THE MYSTERY OF DARKNESS

LET ME BE ME

THE NARROW VIEW

ALL MEN COME TO THE HILLS

List of Authors

Introduction

The world today has shrunk. It is possible to travel to all corners of the earth with relative ease. We see images of other countries, other cultures on our television screens every day. The news is international. We live in what is often termed the 'global village'.

Yet this is not reflected in our literature, particularly the literature available to young people. Most of the books in libraries and schools are restricted to the culture of the predominantly English-speaking Western world. Black and Asian writing, and the achievements of these cultures, is largely neglected.

This collection of poetry is an attempt to change that balance. There is a wonderful vitality and freshness about much Black and Asian writing, and we as editors have tried to reflect this in our choice. We have included a broad range of poetry from every part of the globe, drawn from both well-established and largely unknown poets. We believe that our final selection provides a range of thought-provoking, stimulating, amusing, touching, sad and serious poems which represent only a taster of some of the writing of outstanding quality virtually unknown in the United Kingdom.

Finally, this is a book about people. Not by design, but gradually as the collection grew, we realized that the strongest images, the most powerful messages, were in the people-oriented poems. These poems, with a high degree of emotion and passion, are the ones which will speak directly to all young people, and which we hope will help to raise the profile of Black and Asian writing in our society.

Judith Elkin and Carlton Duncan

Rainbow

Rainbow

When you see
de rainbow
you know
God know
wha he doing –
one big smile
across the sky –
I tell you
God got style
the man got style

When you see
raincloud pass
and de rainbow
make a show
I tell you
is God doing
limbo
the man doing
limbo

But sometimes
you know
when I see
de rainbow
so full of glow
& curving
like she bearing child
I does want know
if God
ain't a woman

If that is so
the woman got style
man she got style

John Agard

A Mountain Carved of Bronze

How curious is language and the web we weave in it
And the sense of colour in it –
What does colour mean to man?
It speaks to him in many languages
Emphasizing danger or seeking friendship . . .

Red of fire that burns or fire that warms
Blue of sea that drowns or bears us on its breast
Black of the storm in a sky still brooding
Or black of the night that brings us sleep
White of dusty earth on a mountain road
Or white of the light that warms and sees.

Black for the colour of mourning
White for the colour of death
Yellow the colour of flowers in spring
Grey the colour of the burnt out hearth
Green the colour of leaves and grass
Symbol of softness and of fertile earth.
Red the colour of blood or passion
Red ambivalent speaks of love or hate
Gold the splendour beloved of fashion
Shadows economy of a nation's fate . . .

Oh the riot of colour in the world of earth
Blackman, redman, brownman, yellow man
Man of colour, man of white . . .
Parrot and peacock, bird and beast . . .
All speak to all in the language of colour
Colours of danger, colours of peace
Colours of friendship or hate or spite . . .

Colour of sun, colour of sea,
Colour of mountain, colour of stream,
Shivering green of humming bird
Thin black wing of hawk
Red of the flaming poincianna tree
Dull mossy brown of alligator's back
Floating by in the silty river
River of fish with silver bellies
And thin black fin of white toothed shark
With pallid under-flesh the colour of lizards' legs . . .

World of colour, world of life . . .
And I saw once a mountain carved of bronze
Stand out against a sky of green, bright green . . .
Almost yellow
But shot with red
Like a Chinese silk . . .

And it came to me that that moment was electric
And never again would I see the hills that bronze
The sky that green and red
The sea that blue, and all . . . gleaming like a parrot's
   breast . . .

World of colour, world of life
World of movement, world of life . . .
Parrot and peacock, bird and beast
All speak to all in language of colour
Colours of danger, colours of peace
Colours of friendship, colours of strife . . .

                                   H. D. Carberry

Moment

Among the dustbins
and scrawny cats
yellowing newspapers
and broken slats
a moment of beauty
breaks in the gutter
as rainclouds part
and the moon peeps
and is caught
in a rainbow puddle
of oil-slicked water.

Cecil Rajendra

Bengali Language (Bangla Beshai)

We speak in Bengali
We write in Bengali
We see the entire world
Through its green glow

We adorn the minarets of our minds
With its countless flowers
Illuminating the sky

With its light in our hands
We journey across the world
Through its sweet melody
We learn the languages of others

Rabindranath Tagore
(Translated by Ms. Anwara Jahan)

Kensington Market

Colours
Colours
Colours everywhere
colours of food
and
colours of people
music sounding
music pounding
Kensington Market on a Saturday morning.

Every Saturday morning
Mom takes her shopping basket
and we go to Kensington Market
Bananas
yams
pumpkin
mangos
okras
and
'whappen'!
Caribbean scent.

Fish with sad eyes
eels
salmon
snapper
and the pretty parrot
Portuguese/Atlantic
Nuts and dried fruits
Mexican herbs and spices
it's Pacos' store
and 'Como estas'.

Chop suey
fried rice
spices from the east
it's Chinese.

The smell of cloves
drifts down the street
it's coming from
the Indonesian restaurant.

All of these mix with music
the sound of
Soca jamming
and
Reggae blasting
'yeah man'!

Colours of food
colours of people
colours of scents
colours of sounds
RED GREEN AND GOLD
Kensington Market on a Saturday morning.

Afua Cooper

Love Letta

Me darlin Love, my lickle Dove,
Me dumplin, me gizada,
Me Sweety Sue, I goes for you
Like how flies goes for sugar.

As ah puts me pen to paper
An me pen nib start to fly,
Me remembrance remember
De fus day you ketch me y'eye.

You did just come off o' tram-car,
A bus was to you right,
A car swips pass you lef-aise
An you stan up stiff wid fright!

You jaw drop, you mout open,
Jus like wen jackass start yawn,
Me heart go boogoo-boogoo
An ah know wha meck ah born!

Noh scorn me lickle letter Love,
Noh laugh after me yaw,
Me larnin not too good, but wat
Me kean spell, me wi draw!

De ting eena de corner wid
De freckles is me heart,
An de plate o' yam an salfish mean
Dat we can never part.

See how me draw de two face dem
Dah-look pon one anada
Well one is you an one is me,
Teck anyone you rada!

Is not a cockroach foot dis, is
A finger wid a ring,
An it mean ah want to married you
Dis line is piece o' string.

Teck it put roun de wedden-finger
A you wedden-han,
Careful fe get de right size, an
Den gi it to dis man.

De man is me. Now sweet-rice,
Keep swell till ah see you nex',
Accep me young heart wile ah close
Wid love an bans o' X.

Louise Bennett

Letter from a Contract Worker

I wanted to write you a letter
my love
a letter to tell
of this longing
to see you
and this fear
of losing you
of this thing which deeper than I want, I feel
a nameless pain which pursues me
a sorrow wrapped about my life.

I wanted to write you a letter
my love
a letter of intimate secrets
a letter of memories of you
of you

your lips as red as the *tacula* fruit
your hair black as the dark *diloa* fish
your eyes gentle as the *macongue*
your breasts firm as young *maboque* fruit
your light walk
your caresses
better than any I find down here.

I wanted to write you a letter
my love
to bring back our days together in our secret haunts
nights lost in the long grass
to bring back the shadow of your legs
and the moonlight filtering through the endless
    palms,
to bring back the madness of our passion

and the bitterness of separation.

I wanted to write you a letter
my love
which you could not read without crying
which you would hide from your father Bombo
and conceal from your mother Kieza
which you would read without the indifference
of forgetfulness,
a letter which would make any other
in all Kilombo worthless.

I wanted to write you a letter
my love
a letter which the passing wind would take
a letter which the cashew and the coffee trees,
the hyenas and the buffalo,
the caymens and the river fish
could hear
the plants and the animals
pitying our sharp sorrow
from song to song
lament to lament
breath to caught breath
would leave to you, pure and hot,
the burning
the sorrowful words of the letter
I wanted to write to you

I wanted to write you a letter
But my love, I don't know why it is,
why, why, why it is, my love,
but you can't read
and I – oh the hopelessness – I can't write.

Antonio Jacinto

About Racism

No matter what the colour of our skin is
we all have something in common.
The colour of our skin makes people
angry and spit on us.
If someone calls us names they want us to be angry.
Hasim thinks it would be nice if people
Said he was their good friend.
Do they think we are animals because we
are black or even white?
Gengis comes from Turkey, he is white.
People call him names.
They say things like 'Turkish delight' and
'I want you for my Christmas dinner'.
There is writing on the walls by the
others about people coming from
different countries,
and the way they talk
and the colour of their skins
and the food they eat.
When we first see it, first,
we feel like writing things about them too
but if we don't it's because we don't know
who wrote those things.
They may be Bengali or English or anything.

If there was writing on the school
about Jamaicans,
we could ask our teachers or the school keeper
to try to get it off
because if a Jamaican new boy or girl
came to our school,
they would think we didn't like them,
and not want to come to our school.

Some of us think we should have more police.
They could stop the killings in the street.
But some of us think we have enough police
And that they can't be there at the right time anyway.
We wish we could share our luck
because we have friends and we can play
and not feel sad.
We aren't all friends yet
but we hope we are coming to be friends.

Gengis, Rahela, Tony, Jubez, Haqim, Zowrul,
Aklas, Aktar, David, Mark, Denise, Denise, Azizun,
Kahan, Kabiz and Ayesha (aged 10)

Smile, Laugh, Sing

Empty Drum

Dere's no wata in de drum
mek hase, go an' get some,
de clothes fe wash teday
so 'urry up an' do wha me say,
me wi sweep de yard till yu come,
for dere's no wata in de drum.

Dere's no wata in de drum
don't badda 'bout no plum,
yu noh ha' time fe dat
fah you hafe wash de pat,
Me wi gi yu piece a bun
when yu put some wata in de drum.

Dere's no wata in de drum
mek sure yu walk back, noh run,
a hope de bucket no leak
like it did last week,
true dat an' de dry hat sun
is why dere's no wata in de drum.

Dere's no wata in de drum
but cheer up, don't look so glum,
an' 'memba noh waste time – go an' come quick
or else me come an' meet yu wid de whip.
what a sigh! yu must smile, laugh, sing an' hum
for soon we gwine av' wata in de drum.

Thelma Thomas

Don' Go Ova Dere

Barry madda tell im
But Barry wouldn' hear,
Barry fada warn im
But Barry didn' care.
'Don' go ova dere, bwoy,
Don' go ova dere.'

Barry sista beg im
Barry pull her hair,
Barry brother bet im
'You can't go ova dere.'
'I can go ova dere, bwoy,
I can go ova dere.'

Barry get a big bag,
Barry climb de gate,
Barry granny call im
But Barry couldn' wait,
Im wan' get ova dere, bwoy,
Before it get too late.

Barry see de plum tree
Im didn' see de bull,
Barry thinkin' bout de plums
'Gwine get dis big bag full.'
De bull get up an' shake, bwoy,
An gi de rope a pull.

De rope slip off de pole
But Barry didn' see,
De bull begin to stretch im foot dem
Barry climb de tree.
Barry start fe eat, bwoy,

Firs' one, den two, den three.

Barry nearly full de bag
An den im hear a soun'
Barry hol' de plum limb tight
An start fe look aroun'
When im see de bull, bwoy,
Im nearly tumble down.

Night a come, de bull naw move,
From unda dat plum tree,
Barry madda wondering
Whey Barry coulda be.
Barry getting tired, bwoy,
Of sittin' in dat tree.

An Barry dis realize
Him neva know before,
Sey de tree did full o' black ants
But now im know fe sure.
For some begin fe bite im, bwoy,
Den more, an more, an more.

De bull lay down fe wait it out,
Barry mek a jump,
De bag o' plum drop out de tree
An Barry hear a thump.
By early de nex' mawnin', bwoy,
Dat bull gwine have a lump.

De plum so frighten dat po' bull
Im start fe run too late,
Im a gallop afta Barry
But Barry jump de gate.
De bull jus' stamp im foot, bwoy,
Im yeye dem full o' hate.

When Barry ketch a im yard,
What a state im in!
Im los' im bag, im clothes mud up,
An mud deh pon im chin.
An whey de black ants bite im
Feba bull-frog skin.

Barry fada spank im,
Im mada sey im sin,
Barry sista scold im
But Barry only grin,
For Barry brother shake im head
An sey, 'Barry, yuh win!'

Valerie Bloom

Richard's Brother Speaks

Richard . . .
What's the matter? Why you not smiln' no more?
You wretch, you bruk the window?
Daddy a go peel you 'kin,
'im a go peel it like how he peel orange.
When Daddy come true dat door,
You better run.
You better leave de country!
'im a–go peel you 'kin.
You bottom a go warm tonight though!
Me goin' cook dinner pon you backside
When 'im done wid you
Richard 'im a come!
Run, bwoy, run!

Desmond Strachan

Alma

'To my second mother,
Philletus Brown'

Al-maa, Al-maa, Al-maa,
lawd ha massy pah me sah
Al-maa, Al-maa, Al-maa
mek hase an' come to me yah.

Yu wait till ah kech dat chile
ah neva know wha she doin' all de wile,
look how lang sense she noh scour de pat
even doh she ha nuff ashes an cocanat trash.

She spen' all har time doin' mi don't know wat
even in a school she dunce like a bat,
dis is all 'cause she soh lazy
an' on tap a dat she soh blasted faisty.

A wanda weh me put de strap
dis yah day she gwine get more dan a slap,
fah de las' time me give har a box
me was de one wha get de shock.

Dis yah too much fa me one fe bear
fah dese kine a boderation har fada won't share,
wen me complain to 'im, all 'im say
dis is homan work, soh me nah get in de way.

But wha' fe do, de pickney outa han'
ef she gwan like dis, she wi neva get a man,
me name gwine be mud ina Clarendan
people a go blame me, dem wi nevva andastan.

35

Al-maa, Al-maa, it noh look like peace me a go get
fah de gal noh reach yah yet,
well, me cyan wait fe har fe wash de pat
wen she come home, she gwine memba all dat.

Thelma Thomas

Oh, My Finger!

Two tiny feet came pattering
Across the bedroom floor,
And then a tiny figure burst
Straight through the bathroom door.

'My finger, oh, my finger, Mom',
The little voice bemoaned,
And held his little finger up,
The blood dripped, and he groaned.

'Oh, goodness me!', gasped Mother,
'What have you done, my son?
How did you manage such a cut?
Oh, gracious me, I'm done!'.

Two bright and tiny innocent eyes
Searched Mother's eyes so wild,
And a little voice ouched all along,
The voice of a frightened child.

'The band-aid, cotton', Mother yelled,
And held the dripping finger,
Then pulled these items from a kit,
She knew she couldn't linger.

'Ouch!', cried the little voice again,
'What day is it, dear Mom?'
'No time to worry about the day,
Hold still your finger, son'.

She soothed and dressed the injured hand.
'Hold still, I say, my son!'
'Ouch!', cried the little voice once more,
'What day is it, dear Mom?'

And soon the bleeding all was stopped,
The finger bandaged tight,
It stood up proudly, and the boy
Felt it a privileged sight.

'Now tell me, son', the Mother inquired,
'Why ask what day it be?'
'You see, I must record this, Mom,
In my school diary'.

Susan Wallace

Little Boy Crying

Your mouth contorting in brief spite and hurt,
your laughter metamorphosed into howls,
your frame so recently relaxed now tight
with three-year-old frustration, your bright eyes
swimming tears, splashing your bare feet,
you stand there angling for a moment's hint
of guilt or sorrow for the quick slap struck.

The ogre towers above you, that grim giant,
empty of feeling, a colossal cruel,
soon victim of the tale's conclusion, dead
at last. You hate him, you imagine
chopping clean the tree he's scrambling down
or plotting deeper pits to trap him in.

You cannot understand, not yet,
the hurt your easy tears can scald him with,
nor guess the wavering hidden behind that mask.
This fierce man longs to lift you, curb your sadness
with piggy-back or bull-fight, anything,
but dare not ruin the lessons you should learn.

You must not make a plaything of the rain.

                                        Mervyn Morris

Worries an' Crasses

Pickney a wha' me gwine do wid yu
me always tell yu 'bout de tings yu no fe do,
but no matta wha' me say
yu always try fe ha' yu own way.

Why yu nevva lissen to me
an' like a gal pickney should see
dat yu should do tings at 'ome
an' lef de bwoy's games alone.

How much time me mus' scream an' shout
fah yu fe lef de marbles dem out,
de time you wastin' playin' wid bwoys
yu should be cookin', yu mus realize.

Wha' mek yu hafe climb de tree
dis ting is not fe gal pickney,
yu work is fe see all de time
dat clean clothes is on de line.

Wha' mek de bwoys yu mus' fite?
yu don't know it is not lady like?
lef de bwoys wid dem cricket game
fah me noh want people fe see me shame.

Pickney wha' me gwine do wid yu
lawd, help mi fe see dis through
fe see yu behave de right way
an settle down like a proper gal someday.

                                    Thelma Thomas

'To Asaniah Tafari Scarlet,
Because you bring me happiness.'

My Beautiful Baby Boy!

Conceived and nourished
totally from love,
protected by Jah above,
now a sleeping babe in my arms,
with all his wonderful
babyish charms.

Suckling so contentedly
at my breast,
that my pen must
surely write,
'oh what a bundle of joy,
my beautiful baby boy.'

Rashida

New Baby

Mi baby sista come home las' week
An' little most mi dead,
When mama pull back de blanket
An' me see de pickney head.

Couple piece a hair she had pon i',
An' de little pickney face
Wrinkle up an' crease up so,
It was a real disgrace.

Mi see har a chew up mama chest
So mi gi' har piece o' meat,
Mama tek i' whey, sey she cyaan eat yet
For she no hab no teeth.

Mi tell mama fi put har down
Mek she play wid mi blue van,
She sey Yvonne cyaan siddung nor stan' up yet
Nor hol' tings eena har han'.

Mi sey a' right but maybe
She can play 'I spy' wid mi,
She tell me de pickney cyaan talk yet
An' she can hardly see.

Aldoah she no hab no use,
An' she always wet har bed,
Mi wouldn' mine so much ef she neva
Mek so much nize a mi head.

Every night she wake mi up;
But a mama mi sorry fah,
For everytime she wake up
She start fi eat mama.

She blind, she dumb, she ugly, she bald,
She smelly, she cyaan understan',
A wish mama would tek har back
An' buy one different one.

Valerie Bloom

The Bugga Man

Mama said, 'Look out for the Bugga Man.
If you don't behave, he'll get you.
In his stiff black suit
And his long black boots
He'll come with his bag and he'll catch you.'

I laughed aloud when she told me that,
But the darkness frightened me more.
I could see his eyes,
I could feel his breath,
I could hear his knock at the door.

Then the gentle wind seemed to cry outside
For the souls of boys he'd won,
For the flesh he ate
And the bones he broke.
I hid in my bed all alone.

The branch bent on my windowpane
Threw shadows like the ghosts of men
Who had come to warn
And to tell me, 'Son,
He's out here with his bag. Don't you let him in.'

Telcine Turner

The Cunjah Man

O children, run, the Cunjah Man,
Him mouth as big as frying-pan,

Him ears am small, him eyes am red,
Him have no tooth in him old head,
Him have him roots, him work him trick,
Him roll him eye, him make you sick –
    The Cunjah Man, the Cunjah Man,
    O children, run, the Cunjah Man!

Him have a ball of red, red hair,
Him hide it under the kitchen stair,
Mam Jude, her pass along that way,
And now her have a snake, they say.
Him wrap around her body tight,
Her eyes pop out, a awful sight –
    The Cunjah Man, the Cunjah Man,
    O children, run, the Cunjah Man!

Miss Jane, her drive him from her door,
And now her hens won't lay no more;
The Jersey cow, her done fall sick,
It's all done by the Cunjah trick.
Him put a root under 'Lijah's bed,
And now the man, he sure am dead –
    The Cunjah Man, the Cunjah Man,
    O children, run, the Cunjah Man!

Me see him stand the other night,
Right in the road in white moon-light;
Him toss him arms, him whirl him round,
Him stomp him foot upon the ground;
The snakes come crawling, one by one,
Me hear them hiss, me break and run –
    The Cunjah Man, the Cunjah Man,
    O children, run, the Cunjah Man!

James Edwin Campbell

The Wheel Around the World

If all the world's children
wanted to play holding hands
they could happily make
a wheel around the sea.

If all the world's children
wanted to play holding hands
they could be sailors
and build a bridge across the seas.

What a beautiful chorus we would make
singing around the earth
if all the humans in the world
wanted to dance holding hands!

Children's Song
(Translated by Chris Searle)

According to My Mood

According to My Mood

I have poetic licence, i WriTe thE
   way i waNt.
i drop my full stops where i
   like . . .
MY CAPITAL LeteRs go where i
   liKE.
i order from MY PeN, i verse the
   way i like (i do my spelling write)
According to My MOod.
i HAve poetic licence.
i put my commers where i like,,((()).
(((my brackets are write((
I REPEAT WHen i likE.
i can't go rong,
i look and i.c.
It's rite.
i REpeat when i liKE. i have
poetic licence!
don't question me ????

                    Benjamin Zephaniah

Innocence

Tell me child that cannot lie
The road to walk and tell me why
The way is paved with coals of fire

Tell me child that cannot lie
Who put heaven in the sky and why
The truth lies in a camouflage

Behind a disguised mirage
So that I cannot find
The way out from behind
A screen that obscures my view
Of things that as a child I knew

Tell me now before too late
Before you meet your certain fate
How I can get to be like you
Show me exactly what to do
I turn to you in desperation
Having forgotten my destination
Each day it gets a little worse
Tell me how to lift this curse

Oh child you took too long to answer
And now I sense you can't remember.

Ngoma Silver

Love

Love,
Where are you,
now that I need you.
I'm tired of
seeing people die;
I'm tired of
seeing people cry;
I'm tired of
guns and war;
I don't want
to hate any more.
So,

Love,
where are you,
now that I need you.

Just a speck of joy
Just an inch of peace
Just a few smiles
the hate will cease

Just a little comfort
Just a touch of pride
Just a pinch of heart
the hate will die

So,
Love,
where are you,
now that we need you.
The women,
The children,
can't live without you.
the doctors,
the teachers,
what can they do.
Everybody today,
needs love to pass their way.

So,
Love,
Where are you,
Now that I need you.
Love,
Where are you,
Now that the world needs you.

Accabre Huntley

Because

when I cried
she thought
there was something in my eye
when I hurt
she asked
if I had indigestion
when I bled
she would not see
and when I said
I need
she walked away
and now
I no longer cry or hurt or bleed
I no longer need
I am emotionally anaemic
All systems shut down
and she says
please love me
why don't you love me?
and I say
Because.

Shabnam

The Hungry Child

Hunger is beating me!
The soapseller hawks her wares,
But if I can't wash my inside,
How can I wash my outside?

Yoruba

The Pond

There was this pond in the village
and little boys, he heard till he was sick,
were not allowed too near;
Unfathomable pool, they said,
that swallowed men and animals just so;
and in its depths, old people said,
swam galliwasps and nameless horrors;
bright boys kept away.

Though drawn so hard by prohibitions,
the small boy, fixed in fear, kept off;
till one wet summer, grass growing lush,
paths muddy, slippery, he found himself
there at the fabled edge.

The brooking pond was dark.
Sudden, escaping cloud, the sun
came bright; and, shimmering in guilt,
he saw his own face peering from the pool.

Mervyn Morris

Fear

Curling fingers
crawling up
the back
of your
brain,
taking your mind
by
surprise,
then gripping
your heart and
squeezing it
of its
life source.
A plunger
pushing
the contents
of your
stomach
down and
out.

                    Deepak Kalha

Mum Dad and Me

My parents grew among palmtrees,
in sunshine strong and clear.
I grow in weather that's pale,
misty, watery or plain cold,
around back streets of London.

Dad swam in warm sea, at my age.
I swim in a roofed pool.
Mum – she still doesn't swim.

Mum went to an open village market
at my age. I go to a covered
arcade one with her now.
Dad works most Saturdays.

At my age Dad played
cricket with friends.
Mum helped her mum, or talked
shouting halfway up a hill.
Now I read or talk on the phone.

With her friends Mum's mum washed
clothes on a river-stone. Now
washing-machine washes our clothes.
We save time to eat to TV,
never speaking.

My dad longed for a freedom in Jamaica.
I want a greater freedom.
Mum prays for us, always.

Mum goes to church
some evenings and Sundays.
I go to the library.
Dad goes for his darts at the local.

Mum walked everywhere, at my age.
Dad rode a donkey.
Now I take a bus
or catch the underground train.

James Berry

Kitchens

Kitchens were places

    we grew up in.
    High-roofed, spacious,

they attracted us
with the pungency

    of smoke and spices.
    From December beds

we hurried to the cheer
of wood-fires, above

    which sang black kettles.
    Once there, we dawdled

over last night's curry
and fresh bread dripping

    from the saucepan, eggs,
    and everlasting bowls

of tea. Discussions
centred on primaries:

    births, deaths, marriages,
    crops. Mother presided

contributing only
her presence, busy

    ladling, ladling. Noise

was warmth. Now in these

cramped spaces, there is
no time for talk. A

   stainless homogeneity
   winks back our sneers.

Chairs are insular;
they do not encourage

   intimacy like slats.
   The table tucks bellies

in. We would not dream
of coming to this place

   to savour our triumphs,
   or unburden our griefs.

Chromium and formica
have replaced the textured

   homeliness of plaster, teak.
   Everything is clean

as a hospital.
The surrealist clock,

   where once the eloquent
   grandfather swung,

clicks forward, stiffly.
We are deferential

to the snap pleasures
of electric toast, and take

our last gulps standing up.

Taufiq Rafat

Hotter Fire

I came here cause I was told
and as a child of eight years old
never knew about no streets of gold
but was unprepared for the freezing cold

Yet colder still the people here
who bid us come and subsidized our fare
and made sure we worked hard for our share
of the freezing cold and the icy air

But a new generation came along
this one stood firm this one stood strong
overstanding what was going down
this one stood up and held its ground

Cried Powell (who first bid us come)
go back! go back! or blood will run
but youth who'd never seen the sun
said 'let it run, mek fire bun'!

And more besides where shall we go
here we born and here we grow
we are accustomed to the snow
and hotter fire is what we know

Well what shall be must come to pass
this snow and ice won't always last
we and they know that it must pass
get ready for the furnace blast.

                              Ngoma Silver

Sweet Mango

Away, here I am,
in search of a country,
trying hard to find myself
a land of fruit trees
to return to,
a sweet mango, perhaps
with my mother's face
on its slowly yellowing skin,
my father's own exile
scattered among the leaves,
my brother's immaturity
and my own
nervously leaping
up and down
on the stones and trash
which hide the roots
from all of us.

                              Andrew Salkey

Black Female Warrior

Tribute to Black Women Everywhere

I am Black
I am woman
nothing can detract
from my strength
from my beauty
from my will

I have suffered all
uncomplaining
unrelenting
I have fought for the future of my family
I strive for the future of my children
everywhere
always

(pause and consider my position)

Enter
the labyrinth of my mind
feel my experiences
encounter the reality of my life
centuries
of pain
of hardship
of suffering
have moulded and formed
my consciousness
my Black heart

Centuries of love
the determination of my mothers
have made me
what I am
Black Female Warrior

Miss K. Cargill

Untitled

Woman
guard well your mystery:
Your own creative fruitfulness.
It is a bloody, an ancient,
and a dangerous knowing.
Beset with chimeras.
But it is the design
drawn on your bones;
the song hidden under your tongue;
the landscape painted
on the inside of your skin.

Barbara Burford

History Makers

Women stone breakers
Hammers and rocks
Tired child makers
Haphazard frocks
Strong thigh
Rigid head
Bent nigh
Hard white piles
Of stone
Under hot sky
In the gully bed
No smiles
No sigh
No moan.

Women child bearers
Pregnant frocks
Wilful toil sharers
Destiny shapers
History makers
Hammers and rocks.

George Campbell

Muliebrity

I have thought so much about the girl
who gathered cow-dung in a wide, round basket
along the main road passing by our house
and the Radhavallabh temple in Maninagar.
I have thought so much about the way she
moved her hands and her waist
and the smell of cow-dung and road-dust and wet
    canna lilies,
the smell of monkey breath and freshly washed
    clothes
and the dust from crows' wings which smells
    different –
and again the smell of cow-dung as the girl scoops
it up, all these smells surrounding me separately
and simultaneously – I have thought so much
but have been unwilling to use her for a metaphor,
for a nice image – but most of all unwilling
to forget her or to explain to anyone the greatness
and the power glistening through her cheekbones
each time she found a particularly promising
mound of dung –

                                        Sujata Bhatt

Your Face (The Washerwoman)

Your face tells stories of
endless strife,
Of heavy burdens and a hard,
hard life,
Where luxury is a forbidden
dream,
And reality tastes like sour
cream.

Your face tells stories of
aching limbs and a heavy heart,
Where joy and relief play no
part,
A world of toil and a world of
woe,
Where little is reaped from
what you sow.

Your face tells stories of
struggle and strength, of
ceaseless energy being spent
Of despair yet hope,
But – like those before you,
You will cope.

For you are like that old dark
tree,
Made of Mahogany,
Whose wrinkled bark and twisted
roots,
Dig deep into the rich soil of
our history,
Feeding you with the strength
of those who have strived
before,
Their Pride, their Dignity,
Their Strength, their Power!

Gilroy Brown

Refugee Mother and Child

No Madonna and Child could touch
that picture of a mother's tenderness
for a son she soon would have to forget.

The air was heavy with odours
of diarrhoea of unwashed children
with washed-out ribs and dried-up
bottoms struggling in laboured
steps behind blown empty bellies. Most
mothers there had long ceased
to care but not this one; she held
a ghost smile between her teeth
and in her eyes the ghost of a mother's
pride as she combed the rust-coloured
hair left on his skull and then –
singing in her eyes – began carefully
to part it . . . In another life this
would have been a little daily
act of no consequence before his
breakfast and school; now she
did it like putting flowers
on a tiny grave.

Chinua Achebe

The Stem of the Branch

None on earth is like her,
She that made me breathe.

None on earth is like her,
She that filled my stomach.

None on earth is like her,
She that knew why I cried.

None on earth is like her,
She that protected me.

None on earth is like her,
She that gave me my first lessons.

None on earth is like her,
She whose death orphans me.

L. M. Asiedu

The Queen

I have named you queen.

There are taller girls than you,
taller, there are purer girls than you,
purer, there are lovelier girls than you,
lovelier.

But you are the queen.

When you go through the streets
no one recognizes you.
No one sees your crystal crown, no one looks
at the carpet of red gold
you tread as you pass,
the carpet that doesn't exist.

And when you come in sight
all the rivers of my body
sound, the sky
is shaken with bells,
and a hymn fills the world.

Just you and I,
just you and I, my love,
can hear it.

Pablo Neruda
(Translated by R. Rowland)

The Executioner's Beautiful Daughter

u revealed nothing   of u
allowed me only
rare glimpses   of u

well rehearsed incomplete
scenes   from u

scattered
                jigsaw
                        pieces
of u

but u left me asking
asking myself
when u   had gone
      just who   were u

      i knew a girl who
      laughed only
      when she was sad
      i killed her
      or so she told me
      in a letter

you know   i never knew you
only pretended to and even then
it was a game
      you know   i never
knew   i would miss you
but i do and dream
of you
      remember you
when i least want to can't
be rid of you
you know   i need you

you pretended to be clever you're not
you pretended to be many things
you're not
too many things   i fell in love
with the woman
you're not.
      what do i do now
      that you're not
      and i know you're not
and you know that i know but still

pretend?

                              Paul Green

Lady in Red

without any assistance or guidance from you
i have loved you assiduously for 8 months 2 wks & a
    day
i have been stood up four times
i've left 7 packages on yr doorstep
forty poems 2 plants & 3 handmade notecards i left
town so i cd send to you have been no help to me
on my job
you call at 3:00 in the mornin on weekdays
so i cd drive 27½ miles cross the bay before i go to
    work
charmin charmin
but you are of no assistance
i want you to know
this waz an experiment
to see how selfish i cd be
if i wd really carry on to snare a possible lover
if i waz capable of debasin my self for the love of
    another
if i cd stand not being wanted
when i wanted to be wanted
& i cannot
so
with no further assistance & no guidance from you
i am endin this affair

this note is attached to a plant
i've been waterin since the day i met you
you may water it
yr damn self

Ntozake Shange

Listn Big Brodda Dread, Na!

My sista is younga than me.
My sista outsmart five–foot three.
My sista is own car repairer
and yu nah catch me doin judo with her.

    I sey I wohn get a complex.
    I wohn get a complex.
    Then I see the muscles my sista flex.

My sista is tops at disco dance.
My sista is well into self–reliance.
My sista plays guitar and drums
and wahn see her knock back double rums.

    I sey I wohn get a complex.
    I wohn get a complex.
    Then I see the muscles my sista flex.

My sista doesn mind smears of grease and dirt.
My sista'll reduce yu with sheer muscle hurt.
My sista says no guy goin keep her phone-bound –
with own car mi sista is a wheel-hound.

    I sey I wohn get a complex.
    I wohn get a complex.
    Then I see the muscles my sista flex.

James Berry

The Weeding Gang

I know the girls are coming,
For I hear the gentle humming
Of choruses they're singing on their way;
I hear their saucepans jingling,
And their cutlasses a-tingling,
Which as their music instruments they play.

They fill the silence after,
With their peals of merry laughter
Which float upon the pinion of the air;
And also ease their walking
With some idle silly talking,
With Kheesaz and boojhowals very queer.

Then once again their singing
They resume, until the ringing
Of their voices mingles with the whistling breeze;
I love to see their faces
With their smiles and subtle graces,
And I love to hear their charming melodies.

C. E. J. Ramcharitar-Lalla

They Walked and Talked

They talked and walked,
walked and talked and talked –
talkative homing dames;
returning from a distant mart
baskets on heads, words on lips –
gossip or tall tales of folk at home.
They clapped their hands;
they screamed from time to time;
they moved their hands in most expressive ways –
their hands spoke even louder than their tongues –
as they swept like a great Saharan wind
along the winding beaten tracks
before them, silent, deserted.
Not even the discordant croaking of the toad,
not even the noise of insects here and there,
not even the songs of birds everywhere,
were heard above the noise of these homing folk
who (forgetful of the ancient saying
that even blades of grass are living ears)
could not restrain their long and wagging tongues.

                                        C. Uche Okeke

My Grandmother is my Love

I love my grandmother with the whole of my heart.
Now she is an old, ancient girl her face has changed,
   of course.
My grandmother of ninety years is my love.
She is a teller of tales.
She is old, bold and always cold.
Indeed, she is never far from a fire-place.
'Makadzoka' she is called, for she once died.
After some time she rose from death.
'Mushakabvudimbu' they call her in Shona – half-
   dead.
My life is in her hands and the life of my family too.
She is a half witch, having been taught to cure with
   herbs.
Her eyes are out but the sense of touch is strong
The sense of smell is there, for she can smell herbs.
Little, thin grandmother of mine!
Looking so young because of eating so many sweets!
Sugar-sucker! Ten teaspoons full in each cup of tea!
My old ambuya! Makadzoka is my goddess.
She hates dirt, noise, quarrels and dry food.
She is ever sitting on her mat in the sun
Or otherwise hunting for herbs.
She is ever smiling, but an egg grows in her mouth
   when
One annoys her.
'I wish to die and rest' she says. 'When will this world
   end?'
'I am tired.'

Beside her is a packet of sugar, a sweet sauce of
   peppered corn.
Her teeth are brown with rust; her nose is sooty with
   black snuff.

Makadzoka is my love, I shall look into her dimples
The laughing dimples are on her chin. They were
supposed to be
Two but there are now a hundred! There are holes
where stagnant water
Was scooped out.

Lovely Mushakabvu
My grandmother
Is my love.

Eric Mazani

My Mother

I

Reg wished me to go with him to the field.
I paused because I did not want to go;
But in her quiet way she made me yield,
Reluctantly, for she was breathing low.
Her hand she slowly lifted from her lap
And, smiling sadly in the old sweet way,
She pointed to the nail where hung my cap.
Her eyes said: I shall last another day.
But scarcely had we reached the distant place,
When over the hills we heard a faint bell ringing.
A boy came running up with frightened face –
We knew the fatal news that he was bringing.
I heard him listlessly, without a moan,
Although the only one I loved was gone.

II

The dawn departs, the morning is begun,
The Trades come whispering from off the seas,
The fields of corn are golden in the sun,
The dark-brown tassels fluttering in the breeze;
The bell is sounding and children pass,
Frog-leaping, skipping, shouting, laughing shrill,
Down the red road, over the pasture-grass,
Up to the schoolhouse crumbling on the hill.
The older folk are at their peaceful toil,
Some pulling up the weeds, some plucking corn,
And others breaking up the sun-baked soil.
Float, faintly-scented breeze, at early morn
Over the earth where mortals sow and reap –
Beneath its breast my mother lies asleep.

Last night I heard your voice, mother,
   The words you sang to me
When I, a little barefoot boy,
   Knelt down against your knee.

And tears gushed from my heart, mother,
   And passed beyond its wall,
But though the fountain reached my throat
   The drops refused to fall.

'Tis ten years since you died, mother,
   Just ten dark years of pain,
And oh, I only wish that I
   Could weep just once again.

Claude McKay

The Mystery of
Darkness

The Mystery of Darkness

The mystery of darkness
Lies in its blackness
The beauty of blackness
Lies in its rhythm
So listen to the rhythm
The rhythm of blackness
And hear the voices
The voices of darkness
LOVE . . . the beauty of blackness
RESPECT . . . the mystery of darkness
HEAR . . . the voices of darkness
AND MOVE . . . to the rhythm of blackness

Lari Williams

Deeper than Blood

Who are we the tawny ones?
Sun-fires, dawn-red, noon-orange,
break in our skin under dusk-shadow
lighting the sepia with intense saffrons.

Are we acceptable to black, and white?
For we are neither, our synthesis
is more subtle. Are both suspicious?
Finding us so dark! So light!

Are we not blended and caught from old
pigments? What new crucible heats
and fuses our proud mixture? Where
are our colours burnt? In what bright mould?

Have we not taken ebonys and crimsons,
Ochres and pale ecrus of loves
deeper than blood for the making of
our harmonies? We the tawny ones?

K. L. Hendriks

Being Black

Being Black means being proud.
To stand and say what you feel out loud
when people's words strip your dignity.
Have no fear.
You have your own mind.
Words can be so full of hate.
We know now there is no time to wait.
At times I feel so alone,
But just where can I call my 'home'?
People fight for pride alone.
One question stands . . . where does it end?
When love wins through?
(Is that a dream?) . . .
Others like me will want to stand proud and free.

Pauline Moure

I am black as I thought
My lids are as brown as
I thought
My hair is curled as I
thought
I am free as I know.

Accabre Huntley

Blackness

Blackness is me,
For I am black.
What mundane pow'r can change that fact?
If I should roam the world afar;
If I should soar the heights of stars;
If earthly honours I attract,
I'd still be black –
For black is black
And there is naught can change that fact.
Africa's my mother's name;
And it is she from whence I came.
That's why I'm black,
For so is she.
Blackness is our identity.
Blackness is what we want to be.
You are white;

Whiteness is you.
My Africa is not your mother,
But yet you are – you are my brother!

A Black Man's Song

I looked in the mirror.
What did I see?
Not black not white,
but me, only me.
                    Coal black face
                    with big bright eyes
                    and lily white teeth,
                    that's lil old me.
Yes I looked in the mirror.
What did I see?
I saw a fella
who's dear to me.
                    Short broad nose,
                    full thick lips
                    and black kinky hair;
                    man that's me.
Oh I looked in the mirror.
What did I see?
I saw a fella
as cute as can be,
                    that must be me.
If you look

in the mirror,
what will you see?

> You may see black,
> you may see white;
> but you won't see me,
> no siree not me.

Jimi Rand

Let's Make History

So we know about slavery
We write about it
We sing about it
So we know about slavery, so we unearth our history
alright . . . what next,
When do we draw the line and say, to the best of our
ability
Come let's make modern history.

Eveline Marius

Africa

Africa my Africa
Africa of proud warriors in ancestral savannahs
Africa of whom my grandmother sings
On the banks of the distant river
I have never known you
But your blood flows in my veins
Your beautiful black blood that irrigates the fields
The blood of your sweat
The sweat of your work
The work of your slavery
The slavery of your children
Africa tell me Africa
Is this you this back that is bent
This back that breaks under the weight of humiliation
This back trembling with red scars
And saying yes to the whip under the midday sun
But a grave voice answers me
Impetuous son that tree young and strong
That tree there
In splendid loneliness amidst white and faded flowers
That is Africa your Africa
That grows again patiently obstinately
And its fruit gradually acquire
The bitter taste of liberty.

David Diop
(Translated by G. Moore and U. Beier)

Historical Rights

To my darling mother and my dear daddy
This is your son Mansfield writing to you
This day to inform you that I have changed
My name from above completely.

Please pass it on to my brothers and sisters
For them to pass it on to my cousins for
Them to pass it on to all my relations each
And everyone.

Mother, father, with you being what you are
'Christian' and me being what I am 'Rastaman'
Saying 'Jah' gave me this new name it will be
Impossible for you to accept but it's absolutely
True and I would like you to believe that too.

Mother, father please try to understand that
'Mansfield Rose' was a burden on my head every
    time
I flashed my dreadlocks.

Firstly I have been reminded time and time again
By English that my name was English. Very strange
I was born in Jamaica. I know no English with a
Jamaican name!!!

Secondly I know no Afrikan with such a name as
    mine.

Address all my correspondence as follows:
Zzaashwaah Jawiattika Sotimjr Blacksheep. Under
    no
Circumstances should it be altered as you have

Re-routed my brain from I was a manchild.

Mother, father I would have really appreciated it
If you had taught me my roots, who I am, where I'm
Coming from, our entire history from I and I was
A manchild.

Jah Rastafari

Jawiattika Blacksheep

Killing Me For I

Mansfield (Scotti) Rose
Yes I knew him well
I had known him for twenty-one years
Of all his friends and relations
I know I knew him best

I remember
We laughed together
We thought together
We ate together
We played together

I remember
We grew together
We worked together
We lived together
We did everything together
To be more precise
We were born together!

Fortunately he is forever DEAD now
I had to destroy him – Permanently!
He was getting out of order
He wanted to dominate my soul
Without asking my permission

Jawiattika Blacksheep

Hallelujah

No STORY – Reality – TRULY!!!

    Babylon!
Mansfield (Scotti) Rose
    is dead!!
        I killed him
    because of I wisdom
I killed him
        because of I knowledge!
    I killed him
because of I understanding!
        I killed him
    for I freedom!!
I killed him
        all because
I am an
        Affrikkan!!!
    despite
        I residency in
    Babylon!!

                Jawiattika Blacksheep

Black and White

Red eyes,
Frozen tears,
Slashed dreams,
Disturbed mind,
Rising high,
Can't face reality.

Fed up,
Given up,
Mus erupt,
Tings tough,
Getting rough,
Gotta bend society.

Face it,
Escape it,
Makes you sick,
Don't quit,
Strike it,
Its been done before.

Link arms,
Working class,
Black and white,
We have a right,
So put up a fight.

Accabre Huntley

Let Me Be Me

Africa's Plea

I am not you –
but you will not
give me a chance,
will not let me be *me*.

'If I were you' –
but you know
I am not you,
yet you will not
let me be *me*.

You meddle, interfere
in my affairs
as if they were yours
and you were me.

You are unfair, unwise,
foolish to think
that I can be you,
talk, act
and think like you.

God made me *me*.
He made you *you*.
For God's sake
Let me be *me*.

Roland Tombekai Dempster

Children of Africa

Children of Africa
our time has come
No longer can we tolerate
the pillage of our heritage
by the white man, the plagiary
of our culture and inventions,
the false indoctrination of our
youth, that results in a
negative self image.
We must organize
and educate ourselves
penetrating the system
to bring down
this racist society
that seeks
to destroy
Africa
and her
people

Makeda B.

A Stronger Wind Than Paradise

Once there was a mighty lion
And the locks of his mane were long and flowing
His fearsome voice roared out in all directions
In a dozen regions dwelled his children
His feet stood north, west, south and east
Indeed he was a dreadful beast
But his children cut his noble mane
And sold it for material gain

Once there was a gentle candle
That burned the wax of truth and wisdom
And all who dwelled within her shadow
Found peace, tranquillity and knew not fear
So the candle burned from day to day
And kept the cold and dark at bay
But an ill wind blew and the wind was stronger
And now the candle burns no longer

Once there was an AFRICA
A land of flowing milk and honey
Her own resources were all she needed
But the devil offered and she accepted
He took her pride and raped her soul
And into slavery her children sold
Now though the name remains the same
CAN AFRICA EVER EXIST AGAIN?

Ngoma Silver

Those Who Spoke

Another race
Of paler face
Built cities on our land.
And with their guns
and rising suns
Proclaimed South Africa's New Age.

The cities grew
On homes we knew
Economies were born!
FISCAL powers
Marble towers
Now ruled our father's world.

A few rose high
And questioned why
The few must rule the most?
Democracy?
Hypocrisy?
Apartheid is the only path?

Teargas clouds
Dispersed the crowds,
Objectors were arrested.
Such ruinous sins
By coloured skins
Must mean another martyred life.

The weary hells
Of prison cells
Became the only world for those
Who spoke their thoughts
Within the courts

About The Way Things Are.

Winds of change
And storms of rage
From Cape Town to Johannesburg
And though they can
Imprison man
They cannot cage a dream . . .

David Mitchell
(Aged 16)

The Ballad of Living Gaol

What men are we – so insecure –
That we can't stand alone,
Unless we stand on other men –
The brothers we disown?
Our skin may shine a different hue;
Our framework's always bone.

Why should a man be locked away
Because he fights to see
A world where everyone is born
With equal liberty;
Though we must pay for life with death
To metamorphose free.

Our world will never be a place
Where wistful dreams come true,
But beauty's still reflected in
The misty morning's dew.
There's hope for what can never be
In the eyes of men like you.

There's hope for brighter futures in
Some distant swallow cry,
Like a shout of exultation
From a prophesying sky
Where transitory clouds of war
Eternally drift by.

There may be hope for lasting love
On a lazy summer day,
Whose joy a prisoner never sees.
Condemned and locked away,
Away from the dancing outside world

In dazzling display.

Politics mean little to men
Who cannot feel the sun.
What's the use of an I.D. card
When we were born for fun?
But he who always subjugates
Is he who holds the gun.

The heaven of this earthly world,
Matched only by its hell;
The angels who exist in it
By Satan's set who fell;
And the happiness we long for
By pain we know too well.

Do not rely on someone else
Or the kindly hand of fate;
Free the incarcerate race of man
Before it is too late,
Release the innocent before
We all are locked in hate.

Emily Taylor
(Aged 16)

The Least I Could Do

One night we were watching the news,
A few seconds of film
A man was beating a girl
With sickening thuds
Of wood on soft black flesh
She was lying down

We did cry.
Hot spontaneous tears, of outrage and shame
And in the High Street, to 'Fight Apartheid',
I gave them 50p
While Mandela gave his freedom.

Anon
(Aged 16)

Federation

Ism schism islandism
Keeps us in a mental prison
Africa Africa lets be clear
All Black people are from there
Compass north star and slide rule
Columbus was a blasted fool
I left India headed west
Ended up in Bangladesh
West Indies is imagination
Doesn't have no constitution

Ism Schism Islandism
Heaps and heaps of slave plantation
Africa Africa far and near
Your people spread out everywhere
And those who drew up all our borders
Stand around like jailhouse warders
West Indies might become a nation
If it turn a federation

Cricket cricket lovely cricket
Marshal tek another wicket
Richards hit a dozen six
The caribbean Africans sharing licks
Any African co-allition
Can only lead to celebration
So dash away the ism schism
Build Africa in the Caribbean.

Ngoma Silver

To an Expatriate Friend

Colour meant nothing. Anyone
who wanted help, had humour or was kind
was brother to you; categories of skin
were foreign; you were colour-blind.

And then the revolution. Black
and loud the horns of anger blew
against the long oppression; sufferers
cast off the precious values of the few.

New powers re-enslaved us all:
each person manacled in skin, in race.
You could not wear your paid-up dues;
the keen discriminators typed your face.

The future darkening, you thought it time
to say good-bye. It may be you were right.
It hurt to see you go; but, more,
it hurt to see you slowly going white.

Mervyn Morris

Encounter at a London Party

For a minute we stand blankly together.
You wonder in what language to speak to me,
offer a pickled onion on a stick instead.
You are young and perhaps forgetful
that the Empire lives
only in the pure vowel sounds I offer you
above the din.

Eunice de Souza

Parting of Ways

Leaving behind the family's hut
where he was born and raised
and listened to his sister's chants

The village one day awoke
bestowed its pastoral pride
and bid him farewell

On his return from England
the neighbours came
flocked round him.
Oddly his first act
was to read them aloud
the opening lines of Paradise Lost
and followed this with a talk
about Longfellow
and his love of Pope

Their startled eagerness
held beyond a reading from Wordsworth

and their eyes lost a little glimmer
as he adjusted his voice
to recapture an Oxford accent

He then unfolded an album
and the village saw for the first time
a grey charm before them
the Thames as it moves silently east
past the Tower Bridge

The village listened patiently
trapped at the edge
of precise
phrasing
unique learning
and there was silence

Some people rose and collected
their stools and walking sticks
parted
and moved their peasant features away
like a squatter rises
recollects himself
seeing his presence
out of harmony
with things

There was an old baobab tree
in the centre of the village
here they went and sat
to regroup back their dignity
here where they know themselves best
in the clearness
of a calm quiet
shade

                    Khadambi Asalache

Dry Foot Bwoy

Wha wrong wid Mary dry-foot bwoy?
Dem gal got him fe mock,
An wen me meet him tarra night
De bwoy gi me a shock!

Me tell him sey him auntie an
Him cousin dem sen howdy,
An ask him how him gettin' awn,
Him sey, 'Oh, jolley, jolley!'

Me start fe feel so sorry fe
De po bad-lucky soul,
Me tink him come a foreign-lan
Come ketch bad foreign cole!

Me tink him have a bad sore-throat,
But as him chat-chat gwan,
Me fine out sey is foreign twang
De bwoy was a-put awn!

For me notice dat him answer
To nearly all me sey
Was 'Actually, what oh deah!'
An all dem sinting deh.

Me gi a joke, de gal dem laugh
But hear de bwoy, 'Haw-haw!
I'm sure you got that ballydash
Out of the cinema!'

Same time me las' me tempa, an
Me halla, 'Bwoy kir out!
No chat to me wid no hot pittata
Eena yuh mout!'

Him tan up like him stunted, den
Hear him noh, 'How silley!
I don't think that I really
Understand you actually.'

Me say, 'Yuh undastan me aw,
Noh yuh name Cudjoe Scoop?
Always visit Nana kitchen an
Gi laugh fe gungoo soup!

'An now all yuh can sey is "Actually"
Bwoy, but tap!
Wha happen to dem sweet Jamaica
Joke yuh use fe pop?'

Him get bex an walk t'rough de door,
Him head eena de air,
De gal dem bawl out affa him,
'Not going? What! Oh deah!'

An from dat night till teday, mah
Dem all got him fe mock,
Miss Mary dry-foot bwoy!
Kean get over de shock!

Louise Bennett

Reality Poem

dis is di age af reality
but some a wi a deal wid mitalagy
dis is di age af science an' teknalagy
but some a wi a check fi antiquity

w'en si can't face reality
wi leggo wi clarity
some latch aan to vanity
some hol' insanity
some get vision
start preach relijan
but dem can't mek decishan
we'n it come to wi fite
dem can't mek decishan
w'en it comes to wi rites

man,
dis is di age af reality
but some a wi a deal wid mitalagy
dis is di age af science an' teknalagy
but some a wi a check fi antiquity

dem one deh gaan outta line
dem naw live in fi wi time
far dem seh dem get sign
an' dem bline dem eye
to de lite a di worl'
an' gaan search widin
di dark a dem doom
an' a shout 'bout sin
instead a fite fi win

man,
dis is di age af reality
but some a wi a deal wid mitalagy
dis is di age af science an' teknalagy
but some a wi a check fi antiquity

dis is di age af decishan
soh mek wi leggo relijan
dis is di age af decishan
soh mek wi leggo divishan
dis is di age af reality
soh mek wi leggo mitalagy
dis is di age af science an' teknalagy
soh mek wi hol' di clarity
mek wi hol' di clarity
mek wi hol' di clarity

                    Linton Kwesi Johnson

From Song of Prisoner

Where is my gold pen?
I want to write letters
To my children
And send them money.

I will not tell them
I am here,
I don't want them
To know that I am
A prisoner,
I want them to grow up
Without suffering,
I want them to pass
Their examinations
And get good jobs
And buy land,
Houses,
Cars . . .

I do not want my children
To get shocked,
I do not want them
To feel sad and sorry
And cry for me,
I do not want them to know
That my hands and feet
Are tied with ropes
And I am sitting
On the naked thigh
Of the stone floor . . .

There is an empty chair
In the cabinet room,
The occupant is on leave,
He is alone
Buried in soft cottonwool
Thoughts of hope
Filled with poisoned needles
of hopelessness . . .

Where is my writing pad?
I want to write
To my parents,
I want to send a fat cheque
To my old mother
And another fat cheque
To my old father . . .
But how can I tell them
That I am shoeless,
That my feet are swollen,
Blistered and bleeding?
How can I tell
My mother that I am
Naked and bruised
All over?

Okot p'Bitek

Free Me Body

Free me body from
de lash and
de pain
of de truncheon wave
when them a tomp me down
and me a roll
on de ground
when them a kick
me head
trying to
kick me dead

When me aclaim borderation
Thatcher are say moderation
when me aclaim brutality
judges are say neutrality
when me are say degradation
politicians are say agitation
when me aclaim compensation
civil servants agive me regulations

So ah say
free me body from
de lash and
de pain
of de truncheon wave
when them a tomp me down
and me a roll
on de ground
when them a kick
me head
trying to
kill me dead

free me body
free me body free me body.

J. D. Douglas

Free My Mind

Free my mind
of its blinkered view
anticipated que
tormented pain
visualized dole queue
party political views
propagandist news

J. D. Douglas

Coloured

When I was born, I was black.
When I grew up, I was black.
When I get hot, I am black.
When I get cold, I am black.
When I am sick, I am black.
When I die, I am black.

When you were born, You were pink.
When you grew up, You were white.
When you get hot, You go red.
When you get cold, You go blue.
When you are sick, You go purple.
When you die, You go green.

AND YET YOU HAVE THE CHEEK TO CALL **ME** COLOURED!!!

Anon U5Z

The Narrow View

I Too Have a Dream

'Won't you help me sing these songs of freedom. All I
ever had was redemption song.'
Bob Marley

I have a dream that one day
Michael Joseph of Handsworth Comprehensive
Sharon Lewis of Toxeth
William Smith-Gordon of Eton
John Bowden-Rees of Harrow
will sit for their G.C.E.
equally prepared
with thoughtfulness
and determination of mind
knowing that the system has been fair to them

I have a dream that one day
successful applicants for jobs
will be judged
not because they have gone to the right school
or live in the right area of the city, suburb, or town
or have the right colour face
but that they have equipped themselves
with 'reasoned awareness'
the right qualification
which in so many cases means the same qualification

I have a dream that one day
the top echelons of the civil service,
will consist of people who are measured not by
their connection to the ruling classes
ambivalent nepotism
the delicate tones of their cut glass voices
or their ability to boast about whom

they sat next to at Oxford
that fair play will not go on inside the minds,
of adjudicators
but will be for all to see.

Until we challenge
the stereotypes
of stilted eyes
the narrow view
of TV lies
perpetual rhymes
of bookish lines
we condemn
ourselves
to perceptions
unreal
assumptions unfounded
judgements unrequested
treatment unmerited
of falsehoods
to the day
we die.

J. D. Douglas

So You Think I'm a Mule?

"Where do you come from?"
'I'm from Glasgow.'
"Glasgow?"
'Uh huh. Glasgow.'
The white face hesitates
the eyebrows raise
the mouth opens
then snaps shut
incredulous
yet too polite to say outright
liar
she tries another manoeuvre
"And your parents?"
'Glasgow and Fife.'
"Oh?"
'Yes. Oh.'
Snookered she wonders where she should go
from here –
"Ah, but you're not pure"
'Pure? Pure what.
Pure white? Ugh. What a plight
Pure? Sure I'm pure
I'm rare . . .'
"Well, that's not exactly what I mean,
I mean . . . you're a mulatto, just look at . . ."
'Listen. My original father was Nigerian
to help with your confusion
But hold on right there
If you Dare mutter mulatto
hover around hybrid
hobble on half–caste
and intellectualize on the
"mixed race problem",

112

I have to tell you:
take your beady eyes offa my skin;
don't concern yourself with
the "dialectics of mixtures";
don't pull that strange blood crap
on me Great White Mother.
Say, I'm no mating of a
she–ass and a stallion
no half of this and half of that
to put it plainly purely
I am Black
My blood flows evenly, powerfully
and when they shout "Nigger"
and you shout "Shame"
ain't nobody debating my blackness.
You see that fine African nose of mine,
my lips, my hair, You see lady
I'm not mixed up about it.
So take your questions, your interest,
your patronage. Run along.
Just leave me.
I'm going to my Black sisters
to women who nourish each other
on belonging
There's a lot of us
Black women struggling to define
just who we are
where we belong
and if we know no home
we know one thing:
we are Black
we're at home with that.'
"Well, that's all very well, but . . . ."
'I know it's very well.
No But. Good bye.'

Jackie Kay

Palm Tree King

Because I come from the West Indies
certain people in England seem to think
I is a expert on palm trees

So not wanting to sever dis link
with me native roots (know what ah mean?)
or to disappoint dese culture vulture
I does smile cool as seabreeze

and say to dem
which specimen
you interested in
cause you talking
to the right man
I is palm tree king
I know palm tree history
like de palm o me hand
In fact me navel string
bury under a palm tree

If you think de queen could wave
you ain't see nothing yet
till you see the Roystonea Regia
– that is the royal palm –
with she crown of leaves
waving calm–calm
over the blue Caribbean carpet
nearly 100 feet of royal highness

But let we get down to business
Tell me what you want to know
How tall a palm tree does grow?
What is the biggest coconut I ever see?

What is the average length of the leaf?

Don't expect me to be brief
cause palm tree history
is a long–long story

Anyway why you so interested
in length and circumference?
That kind of talk so ordinary
That don't touch the essence
of palm tree mystery
That is no challenge
to a palm tree historian like me

If you insist on statistics
why you don't pose a question
with some mathematical profundity?

Ask me something more tricky
like if a American tourist with a camera
take 9 minutes to climb a coconut tree
how long a English tourist without a camera
would take to climb the same coconut tree?

That is problem pardner
Now ah coming harder

If 6 straw hat
and half a dozen bikini
multiply by the same number of coconut tree
equal one postcard
how many square miles of straw hat
you need to make a tourist industry?

That is problem pardner
Find the solution
and you got a revolution

But before you say anything
let I palm tree king
give you dis warning
Ah want de answer in metric
it kind of rhyme with tropic
Besides it sound more exotic

John Agard

Stereotype

I'm a fullblooded
West Indian stereotype
See me straw hat?
Watch it good

I'm a fullblooded
West Indian stereotype
You ask
if I got riddum
in me blood
You going ask!
Man just beat de drum
and don't forget
to pour de rum

I'm a fullblooded
West Indian stereotype
You say
I suppose you can show
us the limbo, can't you?
How you know!
How you know!
You sure
you don't want me
sing you a calypso too
How about that

I'm a fullblooded
West Indian stereotype
You call me
happy-go-lucky
Yes that's me
dressing fancy

and chasing woman
if you think ah lie
bring yuh sister

I'm a fullblooded
West Indian stereotype
You wonder
where do you people
get such riddum
could it be the sunshine
My goodness
just listen to that steelband

Isn't there one thing
you forgot to ask
go on man ask   ask
This native will answer anything
How about cricket?
I suppose you're good at it?
Hear this man
good at it!
Put de willow
in me hand
and watch me stripe
de boundary

Yes I'm a fullblooded
West Indian stereotype

that's why I
graduated from Oxford University
with a degree
in anthropology

John Agard

On Receiving a Jamaican Postcard

Colourful native entertainers
dancing at de edge of de sea
a man-an-woman combination
choreographing
de dream of de tourist industry

de two a dem in smiling conspiracy
to capture dis dream of de tourist industry

an de sea blue
an de sky blue
and de sand gold fuh true

and de sea blue
and de sky blue
and de sand gold fuh true

He staging a dance-prance
head in a red band
beating he waist drum
as if he want to drown she wid sound
an yes, he muscle looking strong

She a vision of frilly red
back-backing to he riddum
exposing she brown leg
arcing like lil mo
she will limbo into de sea

Anything fuh de sake of de tourist industry
Anything fuh de sake of de tourist industry

                              Grace Nichols

Young, Gifted – But Black

When Mebula Ramsandra
  was five years old;
His mother told him, that if he wanted
  to be a big strong man –
He'd have to drink all his milk –
  and he did.

When Mebula Ramsandra
  was seven years old;
His teacher told him
  that if he wanted
To go to a grammar school
He'd have to try harder with his homework –
  and he did.

When Mebula Ramsandra
  was fifteen years old
His lecturer told him
That if he wanted to be a lab technician
He would have to go to University –
  and he did.

So ten years later
When Mebula Ramsandra
  was twenty-five years old,
A big, strong, clever, educated postgraduate –
The man on the other end of the telephone said,
  if he wanted to work for him,
He'd have to be big, strong, clever, postgraduate –
  and white.

Valerie Noble

Just Jealous

'They're just jealous'
My mum used to say to me
When I came crying
Home from school
Saying they'd called me 'nigger'
And it made sense then
Because I liked my brown skin.

But it didn't make sense
In later years
When a man drove his car
At me on a beach
Shouting 'black bastard'
He wasn't 'just jealous'
He was angry that I'd answered back.

Yet I can't say
She was wrong to say it
Thinking today of a black child in care
Scrubbing her skin till it bleeds
Trying to make it white
I wanted to say
'Didn't anyone ever tell you
That your black skin is nice
And they're all just jealous.'

And when my own daughter
comes home from school
Asking why they call her 'Paki'
Shall I say 'just jealous'
Or try to explain
The centuries of racism
That are heaped behind that word?

And will it make more sense
Than what my mum said to me?

Seni Seneviratne

Colour Prejudice

Black boy meets white girl, they hold hands,
At this touch Cupid's arrow lands,
But arrow in the front, or in the back,
It doesn't matter, he's still black.
Her parents give the black a miss –
That, my friend, is Prejudice.

White boy meets black girl, holds her hand,
Visions of a promised land,
Takes her home to see his dad,
Surprise, surprise, his father's glad.
Her mum likes him as well, you know.
Very strange, even so.
This way round they're not dismissed –
Again, my friend, that's Prejudice.

Peter Williams

Getting Along Together

A lot of people are racist
They are racist for silly reasons,
But they shouldn't be.
If they tried to be friends they could.
Just because people are different coloured,
It makes them no different.
People come from different countries
they are all human.
They are also accustomed to different things,
Different ways of living.
We must learn about their way of living
As they must learn about ours
to help make London
Our City
A better place to live in.
It does not matter whether you are
Young or old,
Tall or small,
You are human!
Remember you are needed to make a better city
    For everybody to live in.

                                          Cornnelius Barry
                                              (Aged 11)

A Fairy Tale

Openly he says: Sir, when I grow up
I want to be a fine man; someone like you.
Secretly he says: You old fool, I'll join
a gang like Applejackers or Navarones
and if we catch you in the street
we will break all your bones.
You say you teach me about life
but you don't know that life is strife
between mother and father.

Life is nothing to eat when morning comes;
life is no money to buy books and uniforms.
No this, no that, no taking part
in so many things you say make life.
Life is a drunk father on payday,
and mother with her feller on Saturday.
Life is sickness and no cash for doctor.
What you teach as life is just a fairy tale.

Anson Gonzalez

Building the Nation

Today I did my share
In building the nation
I drove a Permanent Secretary
To an important urgent function
In fact to a luncheon at the Vic.

The menu reflected its importance
Cold Bell beer with small talk
Then fried chicken with niceties
Wine to fill the hollowness of the laughs
Ice-cream to cover the stereotype jokes
Coffee to keep the PS awake on return journey.

I drove the Permanent Secretary back.
He yawned many times in the back of the car
Then to keep awake, he suddenly asked
Did you have any lunch, friend?
I replied, looking straight ahead
And secretly smiling at his belated concern
That I had not, but was slimming!

Upon which he said with a seriousness
That amused more than annoyed me
Mwananchi, I too had none!
I attended to matters of state.
Highly delicate diplomatic duties, you know
And friend, it goes against my grain
Causes me stomach ulcers and wind.
Ah, he continued, yawning again
The pains we suffer in building the nation!

So the PS had ulcers too!
My ulcers I think are equally painful

Only they are caused by hunger
Not sumptuous lunches!

So two nation builders
Arrived home this evening
With terrible stomach pains
The results of building the nation –
Different ways.

Henry Barlow

All Men Come to the Hills

All Men Come to the Hills

All men come to the hills
Finally . . .
Men from the deeps of the plains of the sea –
Where a wind-in-the-sail is hope,
That long desire, and long weariness fulfills –
Come again to the hills.

And men with dusty, broken feet;
Proud men, lone men like me,
Seeking again the soul's deeps –
Or a shallow grave
Far from the tumult of the wave –
Where a bird's note motions the silence in . . .
The white kiss of silence that the spirit stills
Still as a cloud of windless sail horizon-hung
    above the blue glass of the sea –
Come again to the hills . . .
Come ever, finally.

Roger Mais

Legend is What I Speak About

It is legend that I speak about
I speak about my ancient forefather.

He had the alluvial smell
In the hollow of his palm
And on his back the mark
Of an old wound
That looked like the blood-red hibiscus.

He used to talk about the hills he had traversed
About the forests and the carnivore
About the ploughing of the fallow land
He used to speak about poets and poetry.

Every true word uttered by the tongue
Is poetry
Every ear of corn in the ploughed land
Is poetry.

One who has no ear for poetry
Shall only hear the moaning of the storm
One who has no ear for poetry
Shall lose the inheritance of the horizons
One who has no ear for poetry
Shall remain a slave all his life.

When we entered the city
We came upon a total breakdown of ordered
    existence
The mother who has lost her child still inconsolable
    in her grief
The long-limbed youth confused
And the wide-eyed stare

Sightless like the red lotus . . .

I speak of legend
I speak of my forefather
I speak of the armed uprising
Of a people with a fixed goal
I speak of the march of history
Down the corridors of class wars
I speak of history and dreams.

Abu Zafar Obaidullah
(Translated by Syed Najhaddin Hashim)

To Those

To those
Who lifted into shape
The huge stones of the pyramid;
Who formed the Sphinx in the desert,
And bid it
Look down upon the centuries like yesterday;
Who walked lithely
On the banks of the Congo,
And heard the deep rolling moan
Of the Niger;
And morning and evening
Hit the brave trail of the forest
With the lion and the elephant;
To those
Who, when it came that they should leave
Their urns of history behind,
Left only with a sad song in their hearts;
And burst forth into soulful singing
As bloody pains of toil
Strained like a hawser at their hearts . . .
To those, hail . . .

                        Harold M. Telemaque

Brer Nancy

Flamboyant spider-man,
Spiralled sagaciously
In his web
On a cradling calabash-tree;
Strutting on the freckled corpses
Of moth and lizard,
And the wind-blown guts
Of a bumble-bee.
His fragile pot-belly,
Full of laughter;
Conjuring sorceric folklore,
Intuitive
In the magic of his living.

Faustin Charles

Mother Parrot's Advice to her Children

Never get up till the sun gets up,
Or the mists will give you a cold,
And a parrot whose lungs have once been touched
Will never live to be old.

Never eat plums that are not quite ripe,
For perhaps they will give you a pain;
And never dispute what the hornbill says,
Or you'll never dispute again.

Never despise the power of speech;
Learn every word as it comes,
For this is the pride of the parrot race,
That it speaks in a thousand tongues.

Never stay up when the sun goes down,
But sleep in your own home bed,
And if you've been good, as a parrot should,
You will dream that your tail is red.

                                        A. K. Nyabongo

Superstition

I know
    that when a grumbling old woman
Is the first thing I meet in the morning
    I must rush back to bed
    And cover my head.
That wandering sheep on a sultry afternoon
Are really men come from their dark graves
    To walk in light
    In mortal sight.
That when my left hand or eyelid twitches
Or when an owl hoots from a nearby tree
    I should need pluck
    It means bad luck.
That drink spilled goes to ancestral spirits,
That witches dance in clumps of bananas;
That crumbs must be left in pots and plates
    Until the morn
    For babes unborn.
That it's wrong to stand in doorways at dusk
For the ghosts must pass – they have right of way!
That when a hidden root trips me over
    Fault's not in my foot.
    It's an evil root.
That if I sleep with feet towards the door
    I'll not long be fit
    I know it – Yes I know it!

Minyi Karibo

134

Mama Dot

I

Born on a sunday
in the kingdom of Ashante

Sold on monday
into slavery

Ran away on tuesday
cause she born free

Lost a foot on wednesday
when they catch she

Worked all thursday
till her head grey

Dropped on friday
where they burned she

Freed on saturday
in a new century

                    Fred D'Aguiar

Obeah Mama Dot
(Her Remedies)

I

I am knotted in pain.
She measures string
From navel to each nipple.

135

She kneads into my belly
Driving the devil
Out of my enforced fast.

II

For the fevers to subside,
I must drink the bush
Boiled to a green alluvium,

In one headback slake;
And return to bounding around,
Side-stepping bushes for days.

III

A head-knock mushrooms
Into a bold, bald,
Softened bulb.

Her poultice filled
At the end of a rainbow –
The sun above Kilimanjaro;

The murderous vial drawn,
Till the watery mound
Is a crater in burnt ground.

IV

Our rocking-chair counsellor:
Her words untangling us
from bramble and plimpler notions

Into this sudden miles-clearing.

Fred D'Aguiar

The Day Mama Dot Takes Ill

The day Mama Dot takes ill,
The continent has its first natural disaster:
Chickens fall dead on their backs,
But keep on laying rotten eggs; ducks upturn
In ponds, their webbed feet buoyed forever;
Lactating cows drown in their sour milk;
Mountain goats lose their footing on ledges
They used to skip along; crickets croak,
Frogs click, in broad daylight; fruits
Drop green from trees; coconuts kill travellers
Who rest against their longing trunks;
Bees abandon their queens to red ants,
And bury their stings in every moving thing;
And the sun sticks like the hands of a clock
At noon, drying the very milk in breasts.

Mama Dot asks for a drink to quench her feverish
  thirst:
It rains until the land is waist-deep in water.
She dreams of crops being lost: the water drains
In a day leaving them intact. She throws open her
  window
To a chorus and rumpus of animals and birds,
And the people carnival for a week. Still unsteady
On her feet, she hoes the grateful ashes
From the grate and piles the smiling logs on it.

                                        Fred D'Aguiar

137

Terminal

She's withering
before our eyes

and no one
noticeably

cries
We do

the hopeful
ritual

each day
we bring

fresh fruit
we prattle

and we pray
for hours

Her room
is heavy

with the scent
of flowers

Mervyn Morris

Old Granny

A little freezing Spider
Legs and arms gathered in her chest
Rocking with flu,
I saw old Granny
At Harare Market;
It was past nine of the night
When I saw the dusty crumpled Spider –
A torn little blanket
Was her web.

Bonus Zimunya

Earth is Brown

Earth is brown and rice is green,
And air is cold on the face of the soul

Oh grandfather, my grandfather,
your dhoti is become a shroud
your straight hair a curse
in this land where
rice no longer fills the belly
or the empty placelessness
of your soul.

For you cannot remember India.
The passage of time
has too long been trampled over
to bear your wistful recollections,
and you only know the name
of the ship they brought you on
because your daadi told it to you.

Your sons with their city faces
don't know it at all
Don't want to know it.
Nor to understand that
you cannot cease
this communion with the smell
of cow-dung at fore-day morning,
or the rustling wail
of yellow-green rice
or the security of
mud between your toes
or the sensual pouring
of paddy through your fingers.

Oh grandfather, my grandfather,
your dhoti is become a shroud.
Rice beds no longer call your sons.
They are clerks in the city of streets
Where life is a weekly paypacket
purchasing identity in Tiger Bay,
seeking a tomorrow in today's unreality.

You are too old now to doubt
that Hannuman hears you.
Yet outside your logie
the fluttering cane
flaps like a plaintive tabla
in the wind.
And when the spaces inside you
can no longer be filled
by the rank beds of rice,
and the lowing morning
cannot stir you to rise
from your ghoola,
The music in your heart
will sound a rustling sound,
and the bamboos to Hannuman
will be a sitar in the wind.

Shana Yardan

Old man
you sit there
sombre and still
the hair on your head
is now silvery grey
the skin on your face
is no longer stretched tight,
I would like to reach
into your body
touch the dreams
you've had
the things
you've done,
if nothing else
before the lid closes,
look into my face
so if my son asks of you one day
at least
I'll be able to tell him
the colour of your eyes.

                              Pervaiz Khan

To a Crippled Schoolmaster

We hogged the billiard table in your room,
We read your weekly *Mirrors* with delight,
And if some little cretin went too far
Your magisterial wit would put him right.

I still recall your dragging up the stairs
And setting out some time before each bell;
I liked your funny classes (though in truth
I really cannot claim you taught us well).

We watched you crawl from bad to worse,
Drag slower and slower until the term
You didn't walk : your classes came
To see you fade from ailing to infirm.

When you retired from teaching – as you had to,
Your body couldn't serve your driving will –
We built a special house to cage you in
So anyone could come and see you still.

The few occasions when I looked you up
I saw a living carcass wasting slow,
That sprightliness of mind a crudish irony
When all your wretched limbs were withering so.

Without a conscious plan to be neglectful
I didn't seem to find the time
To drop in for your running commentary
On what you called 'the national pantomime'.

I wonder whether time has stolen from me
Something that matters deeply (or should do)
And whether anything I manage now will ever

Relieve my guilt about neglecting you.

And when you die I know I shall be sorry,
Remembering your kindness. But the fear
Of facing death stops me from coming
To see you dying smiling in your chair.

Mervyn Morris

Beggarman

That you should come
Crawling
Like a common worm
Into my yard
Ragged and odorous
Screwing up your face
In unimaginable agony
And with a gesture ultimate in despair
Stretch out your hand
Palm upwards
Begging

Go way, I have nothing.
So much for charity
A barefaced slap
Dazed and puzzled he stood
Waiting
Waiting as if that cracked picture of man
Could storm the barricaded conscience
Waiting with walled patience
Go way, I repeated fiercely. Nothing.
Surprise wiped patience
Hurt, surprise
Anger, hurt
It was done
The unpardonable offence committed
I chased from my doorstep
A beggarman
Hungry

And what of the ultimate insult to manhood
Committed by this scarecrow
Why in this vast and vaunted freedomage

145

Should he
Wearing the rags of his decayed inheritance
Self-pitying, self-humiliating

Face furrowed with a thousand years
Of trampling on
Why come to stand before me
A mocking testament
Even my dog begs with more dignity

You scarecrow in my yard
Your grotesquerie is a lie
Carved on the conscience of time
That we are brothers
You deny the wasted manhood
Coursing your stiff bones
If you want what I have
Earn it
Lie rob burn kill
Assert your right to life
Win the shuddering admiration
Of a world grown weary with humility
But do not, do not
Stand there
A broken dumb image of a man
Palm upstretched
Accusingly
You'll get no judgment here

So he turned away with his hurt angry look
Ill-masking hate
Went out my garden gate like a sick dog
Empty
And in my pocket burned
Three bright red pennies
And in my bones
A twisted agony
Go way
I hate you
Brother

Errol Hill

Beggar

There he stoops all day
Wrinkled
Grey-haired
Senile
With his stained beard, and his pavement bowl.
Hand hopefully outstretched
Entreating
Entreating with his eyes
Entreating with his tongue
Entreating with his hand

Yet we saunter by
Eyes earthwards riveted

Sometimes a knurled stick
Sometimes none
Always the filthy *kanzu*
The tattered *kanzu*
We have observed him sightless
Deaf and dumb
We have seen him piteously hopping
Hobbling and crawling

Still, we ignore the gnarled palm
Still we pore over the drab pavement.

Perhaps he is blind
Pitiful.
Yet he misses not every proffered coin
Though the gesture is silent.

Perhaps he can see?

So we stalk past
So we ignore old age
So we condemn bare poverty!

Amin Kassam

An Old Woman

An old woman grabs
hold of your sleeve
and tags along.

She wants a fifty paise coin.
She says she will take you
to the horseshoe shrine.

You've seen it already.
She hobbles along anyway
and tightens her grip on your shirt.

She won't let you go.
You know how old women are.
They stick to you like a burr.

You turn round and face her
with an air of finality.
You want to end the farce.

When you hear her say,
'What else can an old woman do
on hills as wretched as these?'

You look right at the sky.
Clear through the bullet holes
she has for her eyes.

And as you look on,
the cracks that begin round her eyes
spread beyond her skin.

And the hills crack.
And the temples crack.
And the sky falls

with a plate-glass clatter
round the shatter-proof crone
who stands alone.

And you are reduced
to so much small change
in her hand.

Arun Kolatkar

Myself and I

I thought of myself as an old, worn-out pouch
battered, tattered,
unkempt and in rags.
But I have found that I am not worn out,
but have treasured memories
like diamonds in bags.

To eat, to drink, to breathe, to sing –
it's joy to bring yourself to think of people,
careful and kind,
who restore that precious jewel –
your peace of mind.

Devendranath Capildeo

Life

I do not want to die in this beautiful world,
But live in the hearts of men,
And find a niche in the sun-sprinkled, flowered
   forest.
The play of life heaves like waves
With its tears and smiles,
Meeting and parting!
Stringing together
Man's joys and sorrows,
I want to build on this earth
My eternal home.
Ever new flower-songs I bring to blossom,
For you to gather them, dawn and dusk.
Take them smiling –
And alas, when they wither
Scatter them far away.

Rabindranath Tagore
(Translated by Aurobindo Bose)

Index of first lines

Acknowledgements

The publishers gratefully acknowledge permission to reprint copyright material to the following:

Heinemann Publishers Ltd for **Refugee Mother and Child** from *Beware Soul Brother* by Chinua Achebe. John Agard c/o Caroline Sheldon Literary Agency for **Rainbow**, **Palm Tree King** and **Stereotype** from *Limbo Dancer in Dark Glasses*. King Edward VI School, Handsworth, Birmingham, School Magazine for **Coloured** by Anon U52. Anon from British Defence and Aid Fund for Southern Africa for **The Least I Could Do**. Khadami Asalache for **Parting of Ways** from *Many People, Many Voices* (Hutchinson). Ghana Publishing Corporation for **The Stem of the Branch** by L. M. Asiedu from *Talent for Tomorrow*. Wilfred Barlow and Oxford University Press, Nairobi, for **Building the Nation** from *Introduction to East African Poetry*. Young World Books for **Getting Along Together** by Cornnelius Barry from *Our City*. Collins Ltd for **Dry Foot Bwoy** and **Love Letta** by Louise Bennett from *Jamaica Labrish*. James Berry for **Mum Dad and Me** and **Listn Big Brodda Dread, Na!** from *When I Dance* (Hamish Hamilton Ltd). Sujata Bhatt for **Muliebrity**. East African Publishing House for extract from **Song of Prisoner** by Okot p'Bitek. Black Ink Collective and Jawiattika Blacksheep for **Historical Rights**, **Killing Me for I** and **Hallelujah** from *Black Eye Perceptions*. Valerie Bloom for **Don' Go Ova Dere** and **A New Baby** from *Another Third Poetry Book* (Oxford University Press). Gilroy Brown for **Your Face**. Sheba Press for **Untitled** by Barbara Burford from *A Dangerous Knowing*. Macmillan, London and Basingstoke, for **History Makers** by George Campell from *Out for Stars II*. James Edwin Campbell for **The Cunjah Man** from *African Poetry for Schools I* (Longman Group). Macmillan, London and Basingstoke for **Myself and I** by Devendranath Capildeo from *Out for Stars 2*. Evans Brothers Ltd for **A Mountain Carved of Bronze** by H. D. Carberry from *Caribbean Voices*. AMPS & BASCO for **Tribute to Black Women Everywhere** by Miss K. Cargill from *Black I Am*. Chatto & Windus for **Brer Nancy** by Faustin

Charles from *News for Babylon*. Afua Cooper for **Kensington Market**. Penguin Books Ltd for **Africa** by David Diop from *Modern Poetry from Africa* edited by Gerald Moore and Ulli Beier (Penguin Books Ltd, Revised Edition, 1968), this collection copyright © Gerald Moore and Ulli Beier, 1963, 1968. Chatto & Windus for **Mama Dot, Obeah Mama Dot** and **The Day Mama Dot Takes Ill** by Fred D'Aguiar from Mama Dot. Roland Tombekai Dempster for **Africa's Plea** from *Reading African Poetry* (Collins). J. D. Douglas for **Free Me Body, Free My Mind** and **I Too Have a Dream** from *Caribbean Man's Blues* (Akira Press). Eunice de Souza and Praxis for **Encounter at a London Party** from *Women in Dutch Painting*. Anson Gonzalez for **A Fairy Tale** © Anson Gonzalez; first published in *Collected Poems 1964–1979: The New Voices* (Diego Martin, Trinidad & Tobago 1979). Paul Green for **The Executioner's Beautiful Daughter** from *Smell of Burning* (Trinity Arts Association). K. L. Hendriks for **Deeper Than Blood** from *Bite in 3* (Nelson Caribbean). Errol Hill for **Beggarman** from *Caribbean Voices* (Evans Brothers Ltd, 1966). Accabre Huntley for **Love** and **Black and White** from *Easter Monday Blues* (Bogle L'Ouverture). Edward Arnold Ltd for **Letter from a Contract Worker** by Antonio Jacinto from *Attachments to the Son*, 1978. Linton Kwesi Johnson for **Reality Poem** from *Inglan is a Bitch* published by RT Publications. Deepak Kalha for **Fear** from *Tall Thoughts* (Basement Writers). Amin Kassam for **Beggar** from *Reading African Poetry* (Collins 1975). Minyi Karibo for **Superstition** from *Nigerian Student Verse 1959* (Ibadan University Press). Jackie Kay for **So You Think I'm a Mule?** from *A Dangerous Knowing* (Sheba). Pervaiz Khan for **Old Man . . .** from *Behind Brown Eyes* (Trinity Arts). Penumbra Publications Ltd for **An Old Woman** by Arun Kolatkar from *Jejuri*. Roger Mais for **All Men Come to the Hills** from *Caribbean Voices* (Evans Brothers Ltd, 1966). Madeda B. for **Children of Africa** from *Black I am* (AMPS & BASCO). Eveline Marius for **Let's Make History** from *Charting the Journey* (Sheba). Eric Mazani for **My Grandmother is My Love** from *Senior Poetry Anthology* (Macmillan, 1983). Claude McKay for **My Mother** from *Caribbean Voices* (Evans Brothers Ltd, 1966). David Mitchell and the British Defence and Aid Fund for Southern Africa for

Those Who Spoke. New Beacon Books for **Little Boy Crying**, **The Pond**, **To an Expatriate Friend**, **Terminal** and **To a Crippled Schoolmaster** from *The Pond*, 1973 by Mervyn Morris. Pauline Moure for **Being Black** from *Charting the Journey* (Sheba). Pablo Neruda for **The Queen** (translated by R. Rowland) from *Attachments to the Sun* (Edward Arnold, 1978). Curtis Brown Group Ltd, London for **On Receiving a Jamaican Postcard**, copyright © Grace Nichols, 1989. Jonathan Cape for **Young, Gifted But Black** by Valerie Noble from *Fine Words*. A. K. Nyabongo for **Mother Parrot's Advice to her Children** from *African Poetry for Schools* (Longman, 1978). Young World Books for **Legend is What I Speak About** by Abu Zafar Obaidullah (translated by Syed Najhaddin Hashim) from *All Our Worlds*. C. Uche Okeke for **They Walked and Talked** from *Bite in Stage I* (Nelson Caribbean). Hutchinson Books for **Kitchens** by Taufiq Rafat from *Many People, Many Voices*. Bogle – L'Ouverture for **Moment** by Cecil Rajendra from *Hour of Assassins*. C. E. J. Ramcharitar-Lalla for **The Weeding Gang** from *My Lovely Native Land* (Longman Caribbean, 1971). Jimi Rand for **A Black Man's Song** from *News for Babylon* (Chatto & Windus, 1984). Rashida for **My Beautiful Baby Boy** from *Black I Am* (AMPS & BASCO). Andrew Salkey for **Sweet Mango** from *Caribbean Poetry Now* (Hodder & Stoughton, 1984). Macdonald & Co Ltd for **The Wheel Around the World** translated by Chris Searle, from *Wheel Around the World*, 1982. Seni Seneviratne for **Just Jealous** from *Charting the Journey* (Sheba). Shabnam for **Because** from *Charting the Journey* (Sheba). Methuen London for **Lady in Red** from *Coloured Girls Who Have Considered Suicide When the Rainbow is Enuf* by Ntozake Shange. Ngoma Silver for **Innocence** and **Federation**, and **A Stronger Wind Than Paradise** and **Hotter Fire** from *Black I Am* (AMPS & BASCO). Young World Books for **About Racism** by Stepney schoolchildren from *Our City*. Desmond Strachan for **Richard's Brother Speaks** from *I Like That Stuff* (Cambridge University Press). Emily Taylor and the British Defence and Aid Fund for Southern Africa for **Ballad of Living Gaol**. Pearl Telemaque for **To Those** by Harold M. Telemaque. Thelma Thomas for **Empty Drum**, **Alma** and **Worries an' Crasses**. Macmillan, London and Basingstoke for

The Bugga Man by Telcine Turner from *Song of the Surreys*.
Macmillan, London and Basingstoke for **Oh, My Finger!** by
Susan Wallace from *Island Echoes*. Barbican Books for **The
Mystery of Darkness** by Lari Williams from *Drumcall*. Peter
Williams and ILEA English Centre for **Colour Prejudice**.
Shana Yardan for **Earth is Brown** from *Caribbean Poetry Now*
(Hodder & Stoughton). Yoruba for **The Hungry Child** from
African Poetry for Schools 2 (Longman). Benjamin Zephanaiah
and Thames Television Publications for **According To My
Mood** from *Storehouse*. Bonus Zimunya for **Old Granny** from
Senior Poetry Anthology (Macmillan).